Buster Books

WILDLIFE

A MAP COLOURING BOOK

ILLUSTRATED BY NATALIE HUGHES

EDITED BY SOPHIE SCHREY
DESIGNED BY JACK CLUCAS
COVER DESIGN BY JOHN BIGWOOD
WILDLIFE CONSULTANT: MARIANNE TAYLOR

Welcome to the amazing world of wildlife. The maps in this book will take you on a journey around the globe to discover animals, insects, flowers and plants. Each map is jam-packed with fun illustrations to colour and you can learn about the flora and fauna as you go.

Animals and plants don't recognize the international borders that people create. Some will be found living across vast areas, whereas some might only live on one particular island. The placement of the animals and plants on the following pages doesn't represent the exact locations you will find them, but gives you an idea of the types of animals and plants you would see if you visited the countries shown.

First published in Great Britain in 2016 by Buster Books, an imprint of
Michael O'Mara Books Limited, 9 Lion Yard, Tremadoc Road, London SW4 7NQ

W www.mombooks.com/buster   f Buster Books   🐦 @BusterBooks

ISBN: 978-1-78055-730-4

2 4 6 8 10 9 7 5 3 1

This book was printed in May 2020 by Ruho Corporation Sdn. Bhd., 334 Sungai Puyu, 13020 Butterworth, Penang, Malaysia.

WORLD MAP

ARCTIC OCEAN

PACIFIC OCEAN

ASIA

EUROPE

AUSTRALIA AND OCEANIA

ANTARCTICA

INDIAN OCEAN

AFRICA

SOUTHERN OCEAN

ATLANTIC OCEAN

NORTH AMERICA

SOUTH AMERICA

PACIFIC OCEAN

KEY TO HABITATS
FORESTS
GRASSLAND
MOUNTAINS
DESERT
SNOW AND FROZEN LAND

N
E
W
S

WESTERN EUROPE

Highland cattle have very long, thick hair to help them cope with the Scottish winters.

Carp

Grey seal

Dachshund

British bulldog

Tulips

Chamois

Common kingfisher

Shetland pony

Netherland dwarf rabbit

Berlin

REPUBLIC OF IRELAND

Dublin

NETHERLANDS

Amsterdam

UNITED KINGDOM

London

Brussels

BELGIUM

GERMANY

Pembroke Welsh corgi, a popular pet with the British royal family

LUXEMBOURG CITY

Luxembourg

Paris

LUXEMBOURG

Lincoln sheep

FRANCE

Alpine marmot

A pod of Atlantic white-sided dolphins

Cockerel

Bern

SWITZERLAND

Edelweiss

Monaco

MONACO

European badger

Andorra la Vella

ANDORRA

Red mullet

PORTUGAL

Red squirrel

SPAIN

Madrid

Lisbon

Sunflowers

European bee-eater

Red kites sometimes steal clothes from washing lines and use them to decorate their nests.

Hermann's tortoise

Iberian hare

Iberian pig

Red deer

NORTHERN AND CENTRAL EUROPE

Tufted duck

Barrow's goldeneye

White-tailed eagle

Calypso orchid, also known as 'fairy slipper'

Atlantic wolffish

ICELAND

Reykjavík

Cod

Cloudberries

FINLAND

The Norway spruce is commonly used for Christmas trees.

Pheasant

A red king crab's legs can span nearly two metres.

Western capercaillie

Roe deer

Plaice

Ringed seals

SWEDEN

Norwegian Fjord horse

The two-spotted ladybird is the national insect of Latvia.

NORWAY

Oslo

HELSINKI

Herring

Stockholm

European hedgehogs

Tallinn

ESTONIA

LATVIA

Rīga

LITHUANIA

VILNIUS

DENMARK

Copenhagen

POLAND

Warsaw

Campanula gelida

Crooked Forest, Poland

Prague

White storks like to nest on top of tall buildings.

CZECH REPUBLIC

EASTERN EUROPE

Fallow deer come in five different colour forms, ranging from white to almost black.

Blue tits

Wild pear tree

Wild pear fruit

Poet's daffodils

In the winter, long-eared owls roost in groups called 'owl parliaments'.

European polecat

MINSK

BELARUS

European bison, Belovezhskaya Forest, Belarus

Wild boar

Eurasian lynx

KIEV

UKRAINE

Hucul pony

Great jerboas jump like kangaroos.

European green toad

MOLDOVA

CHIȘINĂU

Carpathian bellflowers

Albanian lily

BUCHAREST

ROMANIA

MONTENEGRO

PRIȘTINA

PODGORICA

KOSOVO

SOFIA

BULGARIA

SKOPJE

TIRANA

MACEDONIA

ALBANIA

Giant peacock moth

Pike

Eurasian ruffe

GREECE

ATHENS

Rock partridge

The olive branch is used as a symbol of peace.

Nose-horned viper

Sardines

Macedonian mountain grasshopper

Cretan white peony

The kri-kri goat can climb up almost-vertical cliff faces.

CENTRAL EUROPE

The Hungarian grey is an ancient breed of cattle.

Eurasian spoonbill

The common torpedo gives off an electric shock when it's under threat.

Degenia plant

In spring, male and female brown hares 'box' each other during courtship.

SLOVAKIA

HUNGARY
● BUDAPEST

SERBIA
BELGRADE ●

The Croatian iris is the national flower of Croatia.

BRATISLAVA ●

VIENNA ●

CROATIA

BOSNIA AND HERZEGOVINA
SARAJEVO ●

Italian crested newts

ZAGREB ●

Carp, Lake Balaton, Hungary

AUSTRIA

SLOVENIA
LJUBLJANA ●

European crayfish

Western jackdaw

Mouflon

SAN MARINO
SAN MARINO ●

ITALY

VATICAN CITY
ROME ●

Dalmation pelican

Alpine pinks

LIECHTENSTEIN
VADUZ ●

Apollo butterfly

Six-spot burnet moth

Eurasian brown bear

Mediterranean painted frog

White-lipped snail

MALTA
VALLETTA ●

European honey bee

Grapevine

Great crested grebes sometimes carry their chicks on their backs.

Eurasian harvest mouse

The St Bernard was originally bred as a rescue dog.

CANADA

TURN TO THE NORTH AMERICA PAGE TO SEE THE REST OF THE U.S.A.

Harp seals

The eastern chipmunk lives in the forests of southeastern Canada.

Canada goose

The Greenland shark can live for up to 200 years.

Atlantic puffin

Columbine flowers

The Arctic fox can survive in temperatures as low as -50°C.

Arctic hares

Wolverines are vicious and fiercely territorial.

OTTAWA

Wood lily

Collared lemming

Walrus

Brown bear

North American beaver

White-tailed deer

Beluga whale

Each snowy owl can eat more than 1,500 lemmings a year.

CANADA

Northern flying squirrel

Maple leaf

Maple syrup is made by boiling the sap of the maple tree.

Dall sheep

Grey wolf

Canada lynx

UNITED STATES OF AMERICA (ALASKA)

Pink salmon often return to the river they were born in to reproduce.

Killer whale (Orca)

Moose lose their antlers in the winter and they grow new ones in the spring.

NORTH AMERICA

Blue crab

Bottle-nosed dolphins

Great white sharks can have up to seven rows of razor-sharp teeth.

American toad

Raccoon

WASHINGTON D.C.

Eastern Hercules beetle

Red cardinals

Alligator

Monarch butterflies migrate to Mexico in the autumn.

The American bald eagle is the national bird of the U.S.A.

Coyotes

American black bears

Wild turkey

American bison

Black-tailed prairie dogs live in underground 'towns'.

Texas longhorn

Black-tailed jackrabbit

Mustang horse

UNITED STATES OF AMERICA

Rocky Mountains elk

Joshua trees

Gila monster, a venomous lizard

I'iwi birds

The striped skunk emits a foul-smelling liquid when it's under threat.

Mountain beavers

Sequoias are the tallest trees in the world.

Saguaro cactus

Western diamondback rattlesnake

Hawaiian green sea turtle

HAWAII (THE MOST RECENT AMERICAN STATE) IS IN THE PACIFIC OCEAN, THOUSANDS OF MILES AWAY FROM THE REST OF THE U.S.A.

CENTRAL AMERICA

The leatherback sea turtle is the largest turtle on Earth.

Longsnout seahorse

Yellowtail damselfish

White-nosed coati

West Indian manatee

Atlantic sailfish

THE BAHAMAS
NASSAU

DOMINICAN REPUBLIC
SANTO DOMINGO

ANTIGUA & BARBUDA
ST JOHN'S

St KITTS & NEVIS
BASSETERRE

DOMINICA
ROSEAU

St LUCIA
CASTRIES

BARBADOS
BRIDGETOWN

St VINCENT & THE GRENADINES
KINGSTOWN

GRENADA
St GEORGE'S

TRINIDAD & TOBAGO
PORT-OF-SPAIN

French angelfish

The Hercules beetle can lift 850 times its body weight.

HAITI
PORT AU PRINCE

(female)

Resplendent quetzal

(male)

Puma (Cougar)

Collared peccary

Cownose ray

CUBA
HAVANA

JAMAICA
KINGSTON

Tomtate grunt

Roseate spoonbills have bright pink plumage.

Central American coral snake

Guatemalan black howler monkeys

Golden barrel cactus

Mexican passionflowers

MEXICO
MEXICO CITY

BELIZE
BELMOPAN

HONDURAS
TEGUCIGALPA

GUATEMALA
GUATEMALA CITY

NICARAGUA
MANAGUA

COSTA RICA
SAN JOSÉ

PANAMA
PANAMA CITY

EL SALVADOR
SAN SALVADOR

Paca

The chocolate cosmos flower has a chocolatey scent.

Mexican salamanders (Axolotls)

Maquilishuat, the national tree of El Salvador

The green basilisk lizard can run on water at a speed of 1.5 metres per second.

A school of hammerhead sharks

Strawberry poison dart frog

SOUTH AMERICA

Queen conch

Orinoco crocodile

A giant anteater eats around 35,000 ants a day.

Amazonian royal flycatcher

VENEZUELA
CARACAS

Bromeliad

COLOMBIA

BOGOTA

GUYANA
GEORGETOWN
PARAMARIBO
SURINAME

Boa constrictors can grow up to four metres long.

Scarlet macaw

Pink river dolphins

Hawksbill sea turtle

The Amazon is the largest tropical rainforest in the world.

BRAZIL

Jaguar

Rubber tree

The Brazilian three-banded armadillo can roll itself into a ball.

Blue morpho butterfly

Piranha

South American tapirs

Harpy eagle

BRASÍLIA

Blue-bellied parrot

Toco toucan

The three-toed sloth is the world's slowest mammal.

Heliconia plant

Scarlet ibis

Acai berries

Yellow-banded poison dart frog

Common vampire bat

Cocoa seeds are used to make chocolate.

Golden lion tamarins

Spotted eagle ray

South American sea lion

Cocoa tree

Humpback whale

SOUTH AMERICA

MOST OF THE SPECIES ON THE GALÁPAGOS ISLANDS ARE ENDEMIC (NOT FOUND ANYWHERE ELSE IN THE WORLD).

The Galápagos tortoise can live for 150 years.

Wrinkle-faced bat

ECUADOR
Quito

Blue-footed boobies

Marine iguana

Male Darwin's beetles use their over-sized jaws to fight.

Monkey puzzle tree

Blue-and-yellow macaws

Northern glass frog

Lima
PERU

The Andean condor is one of the heaviest birds that can fly.

Cantuta, also known as 'the sacred flower of the Incas'

BOLIVIA
La Paz
Sucre

Spectacled bear

The kinkajou can run quickly in either direction by turning its feet backwards.

Marvellous spatuletail hummingbirds

CHILE

PARAGUAY
Asunción

The bushmaster snake can survive on fewer than ten meals a year.

Capybaras

Yacare caiman

Giant oarfish live in deep waters and can grow up to 17 metres long.

Santiago

Shorthorn cattle

Buenos Aires
URUGUAY
Montevideo

Alpaca

ARGENTINA

The Southern pudú is the smallest deer species in the world.

Llama

South Andean deer

Southern pudú fawn

Atlantic blue marlin

Greater rhea

Humboldt penguins

Killer whale (Orca)

EAST ASIA

Japanese macaque monkeys enjoy bathing in hot volcanic springs.

The Amami rabbit only lives on two tiny Japanese islands.

JAPAN

Tokyo

White-crested laughingthrush

Japanese spider crab

Blue-ringed octopus

NORTH KOREA

Pyongyang

SOUTH KOREA

Seoul

Mandarinfish

TAIWAN

Taipei

There are fewer than 2,000 giant pandas alive in the wild.

Korean fir

Beijing

Bamboo

Sika deer

Peony

Asian black bear, also known as 'moon bear'

Grass puffer

Raccoon dog

Chrysanthemum

Tea

CHINA

Chinese giant salamander

Golden takin

The Chinese pangolin has big scales on its body rather than fur.

Golden pheasant

(male)

(female)

Marbled polecat

Red panda

The Chinese paddlefish is called 'the giant panda of the river', because it is so rare.

SOUTHEAST ASIA

Indochinese tiger

Greater mouse-deer

Tamaraw

Roosevelt's muntjac

The Komodo dragon is the heaviest lizard on Earth.

Giant golden-crowned flying fox

Red-breasted parakeet

The Philippine eagle is one of the biggest birds of prey in the world.

Flying gurnard

Rafflesia arnoldii is the largest flower in the world.

The male great argus spreads its wings like an umbrella and dances around to attract a mate.

Pearl gourami

EAST TIMOR

DILI

PHILIPPINES

MANILA

Wagler's pit viper

Timor monitor

INDONESIA

Proboscis monkey

Clouded leopard

VIETNAM

Blue-eared Kingfisher

BANDAR SERI BEGAWAN

BRUNEI

Rhinoceros hornbill

MALAYSIA

False gharial

HANOI

LAOS

VIENTIANE

THAILAND

BANGKOK

CAMBODIA

PHNOM PENH

Red-shanked douc

KUALA LUMPUR

SINGAPORE

SINGAPORE

JAKARTA

Orangutans

MYANMAR (BURMA)

NAYPYIDAW

Sun bear

Babirusa

Tokay gecko

Malayan tapirs can move their noses around like miniature elephant trunks.

NORTH ASIA

The Ural owl can knock someone over with the force of its swoop.

Kamchatka brown bear

Amur leopard

South Russian tarantula

Pollack

Magnificent viper

Bohemian waxwing

Steller's sea eagle

Arnica montana flower

Mongolian accentor

The Pallas's cat is very fluffy to keep it warm on cold nights in the desert.

Markhor

Lion's mane jellyfish

Baikal seal, Lake Baikal

RUSSIA

Ulan Bator ●

MONGOLIA

Serotine bat

Bactrian camel

Siberian crane

Eurasian hamster

Snow sheep

Edelweiss

KYRGYZSTAN

Bishkek ●

Astana ●

Tashkent ●

TAJIKISTAN

Buchara shrew

KAZAKHSTAN

Dushanbe ●

Siberian tiger

● Moscow

UZBEKISTAN

TURKMENISTAN

Ashgabat ●

Spoon-billed sandpiper

The saiga antelope's big nose helps warm up the air it breathes, so its lungs don't get chilled.

Black goby

Chamomile flowers

The honey badger is one of the fiercest and most fearless animals in the world.

SOUTH ASIA

Golden langur

Bengal tiger

Indian leopard

Male nilgais fight by headbutting, and hitting each other with their necks.

Himalayan blue sheep

Hump-nosed lizard

Rhododendron

BHUTAN
THIMPHU

DHAKA

BANGLADESH

Indian rhinoceros

Eclipse parrotfish

SRI LANKA

COLOMBO
SRI JAYAWARDENEPURA KOTTE

Blue water lily

Chestnut-backed owlet

Himalayan monal

NEPAL
KATHMANDU

Afghan hound

NEW DELHI

PAKISTAN
ISLAMABAD

AFGHANISTAN

Afghan snowfinch
KABUL

Leaf insect

Indian elephant

INDIA

Lion-tailed macaque

Indus river dolphin

Slender loris, also known as 'Kaadu Paapa', which means 'forest baby'

MALDIVES
MALE

Coconut crabs are the biggest crabs in the world. They live on land and can climb trees.

Woolly flying squirrel

Marco Polo sheep

Sand cat

Indian peafowl

Squat lobster

Laggerhead turtles can weigh as much as 1,000 kg.

SOUTHWEST ASIA

Israeli fan-fingered gecko

Gaittered gazelle

The silver-washed fritillary has a beautiful courtship 'dance'. The male flies in loops around the female.

A dugong can weigh more than 1,000 kg, but its brain only weighs 300 grams.

Caracal

Common fig

Yellow-bellied sea snake

Sawfish

Arabian camels

Blue-cheeked bee-eaters

IRAN

MUSCAT

OMAN

ABU DHABI

UNITED ARAB EMIRATES

DOHA

QATAR

KUWAIT

BAHRAIN

MANAMA

RIYADH

SAUDI ARABIA

YEMEN

SANA'A

Poppy anemone

TEHRAN

BAKU

GEORGIA

TBILISI

ARMENIA

YEREVAN

AZERBAIJAN

BAGHDAD

IRAQ

KUWAIT

Turkish pines

Pistachio

The dragon's blood tree gets its name from its bright red sap.

Angora goat

TURKEY

ANKARA

NICOSIA

CYPRUS

BEIRUT

LEBANON

SYRIA

DAMASCUS

JERUSALEM

ISRAEL

AMMAN

JORDAN

Bezoar ibex

Spiny-tailed agama

Arabian cobra

Grey-headed swamphen

Hoopoe

Common chameleon

Sinai agama

In parts of Asia, striped hyenas symbolise love and faithfulness.

There may be fewer than 100 Asiatic cheetahs left in the wild.

Greater flamingo

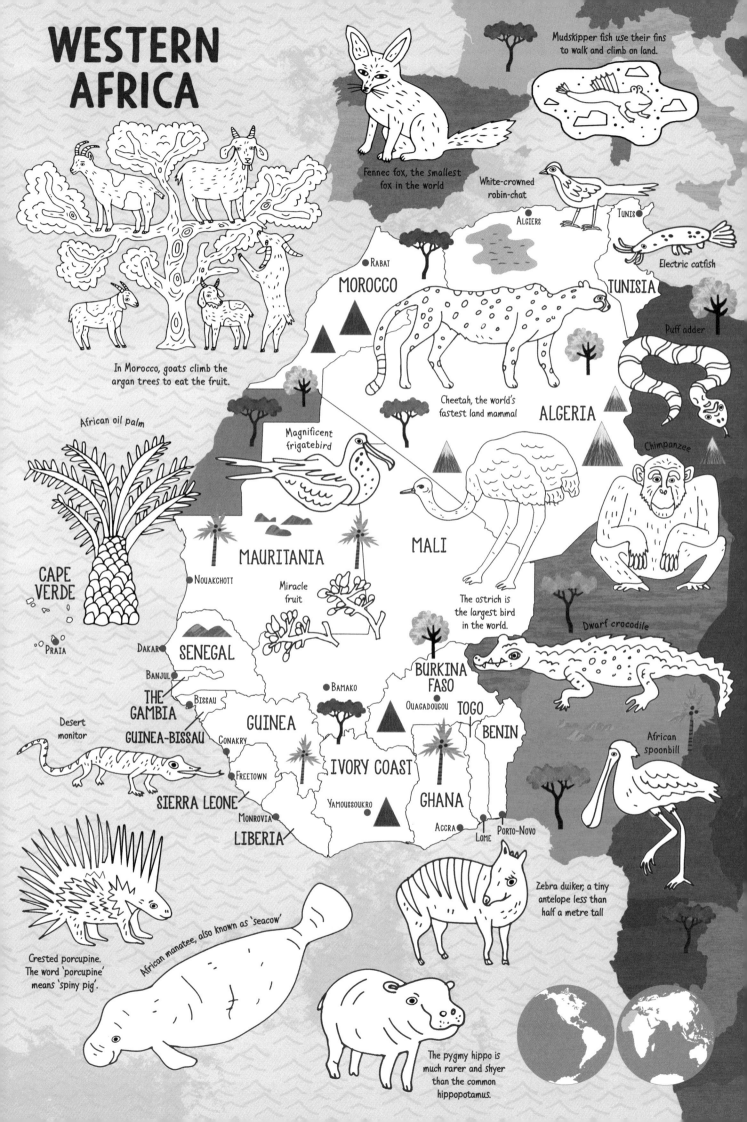

WESTERN AFRICA

In Morocco, goats climb the argan trees to eat the fruit.

Fennec fox, the smallest fox in the world

Mudskipper fish use their fins to walk and climb on land.

White-crowned robin-chat

Electric catfish

Puff adder

African oil palm

Magnificent frigatebird

Cheetah, the world's fastest land mammal

MOROCCO

• Rabat

ALGIERS

TUNIS

TUNISIA

ALGERIA

Chimpanzee

MAURITANIA

• NOUAKCHOTT

Miracle fruit

MALI

The ostrich is the largest bird in the world.

Dwarf crocodile

CAPE VERDE

°° PRAIA

SENEGAL

DAKAR •

BANJUL •

THE GAMBIA

BISSAU •

GUINEA-BISSAU

• BAMAKO

BURKINA FASO

OUAGADOUGOU

TOGO

BENIN

African spoonbill

Desert monitor

GUINEA

CONAKRY •

IVORY COAST

GHANA

FREETOWN •

SIERRA LEONE

YAMOUSSOUKRO •

MONROVIA •

LIBERIA

ACCRA •

LOME •

PORTO-NOVO •

Zebra duiker, a tiny antelope less than half a metre tall

Crested porcupine. The word 'porcupine' means 'spiny pig'.

African manatee, also known as 'seacow'

The pygmy hippo is much rarer and shyer than the common hippopotamus.

EASTERN AFRICA

Lesser flamingos perform a spectacular courtship dance.

Leopard

Tiger shark

Female bluespotted ribbontail rays may be pregnant for as long as 12 months.

Superb starling

The sausage tree's fruits are poisonous.

Egyptian lotus

ERITREA — ASMARA

DJIBOUTI — DJIBOUTI

SOMALIA — MOGADISHU

ETHIOPIA — ADDIS ABABA

Frankincense resin is used in incense and perfumes.

KENYA — NAIROBI

Scarab (dung) beetle

EGYPT — CAIRO

Black mamba, one of the world's deadliest snakes

SUDAN — KHARTOUM

Frankincense tree

SOUTH SUDAN — JUBA

UGANDA — KAMPALA

Mountain gorilla, Bwindi Impenetrable National Park, Uganda

Flame lily

Red river hog

LIBYA — TRIPOLI

Kirk's dik-dik

CHAD — N'DJAMENA

Grey crowned crane

CENTRAL AFRICAN REPUBLIC — BANGUI

Red-tailed monkey

Lilac-breasted roller

Greater kudu

Desert hedgehog

NIGER — NIAMEY

NIGERIA — ABUJA

CAMEROON — YAOUNDE

EQUITORIAL GUINEA — MALABO

Yellow baboon with baby

The red-and-yellow barbet nests in termite mounds.

Mandrill

Baobabs, also known as upside-down trees

Spiny lobster

The basking shark is one of the biggest sharks in the world, but it only feeds on tiny plankton.

SOUTHERN AFRICA

Lions live in groups called prides.

Warthogs can survive without water for several months.

Southern red bishop

African buffalo

African rock python

São Tomé

Libreville

SÃO TOMÉ AND PRÍNCIPE

GABON

REPUBLIC OF CONGO

RWANDA

Kigali

BURUNDI

Bujumbura

TANZANIA

Rooibos plant

Brazzaville

DEMOCRATIC REPUBLIC OF CONGO

Kinshasa

Dodoma

Leatherback turtle

ANGOLA

African elephants

Zebra

South African giraffe

Luanda

Black rhinoceros

SEYCHELLES

Victoria

COMOROS

Moroni

ANGOLA

Impala

ZAMBIA

MALAWI

Lilongwe

MOZAMBIQUE

Giraffe weevil

King protea

Lusaka

Antananarivo

Harare

ZIMBABWE

NAMIBIA

Spotted hyena

MADAGASCAR

Hippopotamus is Greek for 'river horse'.

Windhoek

BOTSWANA

Gaborone

Maputo

The silky sifaka is one of the rarest mammals on Earth.

Mbabane

SWAZILAND

PORT LOUIS

MAURITIUS

Cape grey mongoose

Maseru

LESOTHO

SOUTH AFRICA

Cape Town

African dwarf frog

The black wildebeest can run at speeds of 80 km an hour.

African penguins

Cape fur seals

The whale shark is the largest fish in the world.

AUSTRALIA

AUSTRALIA

CANBERRA

The Great Barrier Reef is the largest coral reef in the world. Over 1,500 fish species live here.

Reef fish

Coral

Sea anemones catch their food in their long, waving tentacles.

Possums

Sydney funnel-web, the deadliest spider in Australia

Koalas sleep for up to 18 hours a day.

Little red flying fox

Ulysses butterfly

Saltwater crocodile

Cassowary

Wombat

Long-nosed bandicoot

The Kookaburra makes a laughter-like sound.

Box jellyfish are one of the deadliest marine animals. Each tentacle has around 5,000 sting cells.

Frilled lizard

Australian green tree frog

Eucalyptus

Weedy seadragon

Bottlenose dolphins

Red kangaroos can travel eight metres in a single leap.

Dingo

Australian sea lion

The red lionfish has venom in its long spines to protect it from predators.

Manta ray

Emu

Tiger snake

Kangaroo paw

The thorny devil has a 'false head' on its shoulders that it uses as a decoy when threatened.

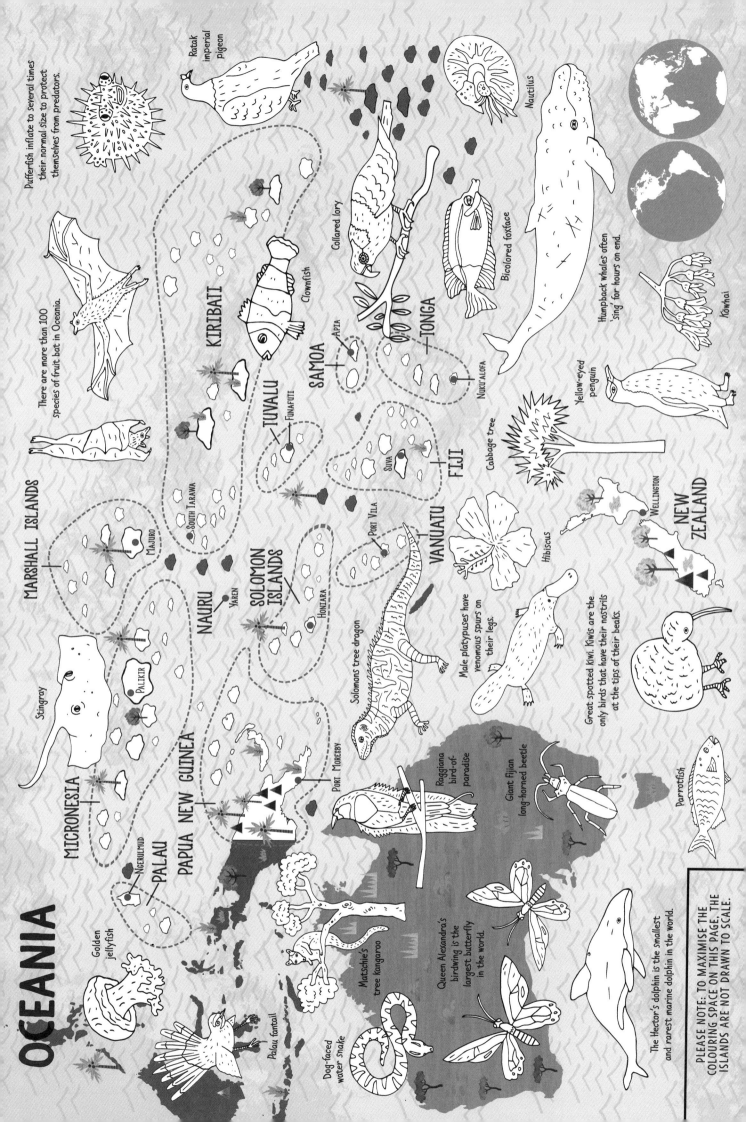

OCEANIA

Pufferfish inflate to several times their normal size to protect themselves from predators.

There are more than 100 species of fruit bat in Oceania.

Ratak imperial pigeon

Nautilus

Collared lory

Bicolored foxface

Humpback whales often 'sing' for hours on end.

Kōwhai

Yellow-eyed penguin

Clownfish

KIRIBATI

SAMOA
APIA

TONGA
NUKU'ALOFA

TUVALU
FUNAFUTI

FIJI
SUVA

Cabbage tree

MARSHALL ISLANDS
MAJURO

SOUTH TARAWA

VANUATU
PORT VILA

Hibiscus

NEW ZEALAND
WELLINGTON

NAURU
YAREN

SOLOMON ISLANDS
HONIARA

Solomons tree dragon

Male platypuses have venomous spurs on their legs.

Great spotted kiwi. Kiwis are the only birds that have their nostrils at the tips of their beaks.

Stingray

MICRONESIA

PAPUA NEW GUINEA
PORT MORESBY

Raggiana bird-of-paradise

Giant Fijian long-horned beetle

Parrotfish

NGERULMUD
PALAU
PALIKIR

Golden jellyfish

Palau fantail

Dog-faced water snake

Matschie's tree kangaroo

Queen Alexandra's birdwing is the largest butterfly in the world.

The Hector's dolphin is the smallest and rarest marine dolphin in the world.

PLEASE NOTE: TO MAXIMISE THE COLOURING SPACE ON THIS PAGE, THE ISLANDS ARE NOT DRAWN TO SCALE.

ANTARCTICA

The sea pig lives in the coldest, deepest parts of the ocean.

Weddell seals

The mackerel icefish has colourless blood.

Krill live in large groups called swarms.

Antarctic pearlwort

The wandering albatross has the biggest wingspan of any bird.

South polar skua

The male southern elephant seal has a trunklike inflatable snout.

Adélie penguins

Rockhopper penguin

Colossal squid

Hourglass dolphin

Emperor penguins

The blue whale is the largest animal ever to have lived on Earth.

ARCTIC

Purple saxifrage

Long-tailed duck

Black crowberry

Arctic poppy

Arctic lupine

Polar bears have an amazing sense of smell. They can sniff out prey up to 16 km away.

Every year the Arctic tern migrates from the Arctic to Antarctica.

Arctic wolf

The bowhead whale has the largest mouth of any animal.

Reindeer

Lemming

Reindeer lichen

Gyrfalcon

Musk-ox

Arctic redpoll

Hooded seal

Narwhal, often called 'the unicorn of the sea'

FLAGS OF THE WORLD
COLOUR IN THE FLAGS THE SAME SHADE AS THE COLOURED DOTS.

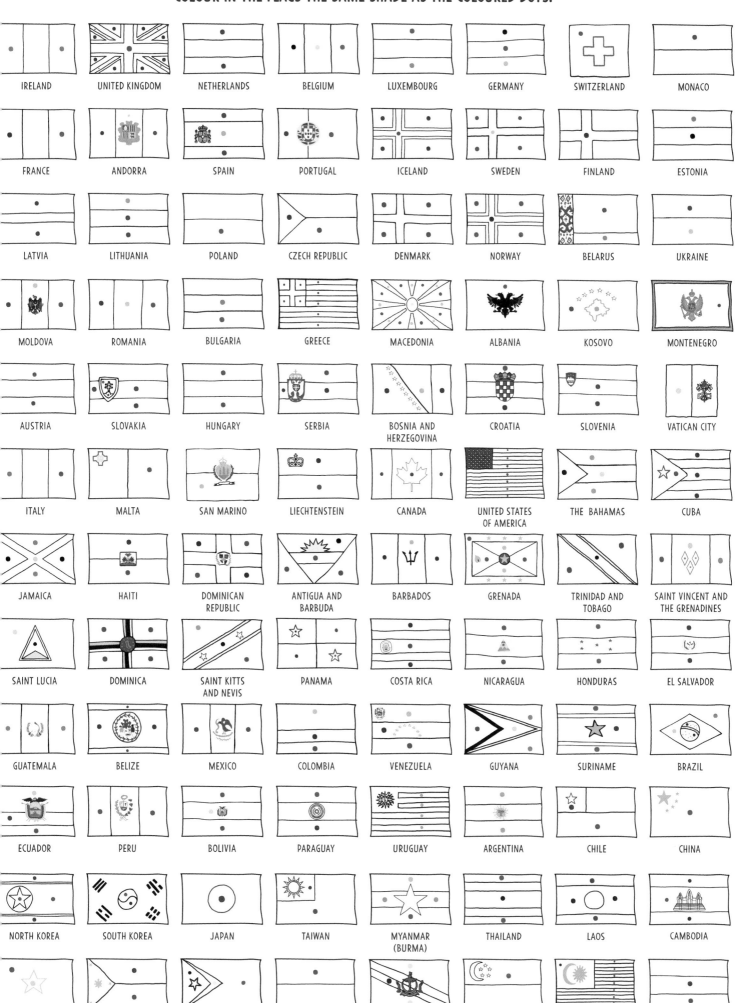

IRELAND   UNITED KINGDOM   NETHERLANDS   BELGIUM   LUXEMBOURG   GERMANY   SWITZERLAND   MONACO

FRANCE   ANDORRA   SPAIN   PORTUGAL   ICELAND   SWEDEN   FINLAND   ESTONIA

LATVIA   LITHUANIA   POLAND   CZECH REPUBLIC   DENMARK   NORWAY   BELARUS   UKRAINE

MOLDOVA   ROMANIA   BULGARIA   GREECE   MACEDONIA   ALBANIA   KOSOVO   MONTENEGRO

AUSTRIA   SLOVAKIA   HUNGARY   SERBIA   BOSNIA AND HERZEGOVINA   CROATIA   SLOVENIA   VATICAN CITY

ITALY   MALTA   SAN MARINO   LIECHTENSTEIN   CANADA   UNITED STATES OF AMERICA   THE BAHAMAS   CUBA

JAMAICA   HAITI   DOMINICAN REPUBLIC   ANTIGUA AND BARBUDA   BARBADOS   GRENADA   TRINIDAD AND TOBAGO   SAINT VINCENT AND THE GRENADINES

SAINT LUCIA   DOMINICA   SAINT KITTS AND NEVIS   PANAMA   COSTA RICA   NICARAGUA   HONDURAS   EL SALVADOR

GUATEMALA   BELIZE   MEXICO   COLOMBIA   VENEZUELA   GUYANA   SURINAME   BRAZIL

ECUADOR   PERU   BOLIVIA   PARAGUAY   URUGUAY   ARGENTINA   CHILE   CHINA

NORTH KOREA   SOUTH KOREA   JAPAN   TAIWAN   MYANMAR (BURMA)   THAILAND   LAOS   CAMBODIA

VIETNAM   PHILIPPINES   EAST TIMOR   INDONESIA   BRUNEI   SINGAPORE   MALAYSIA   RUSSIA

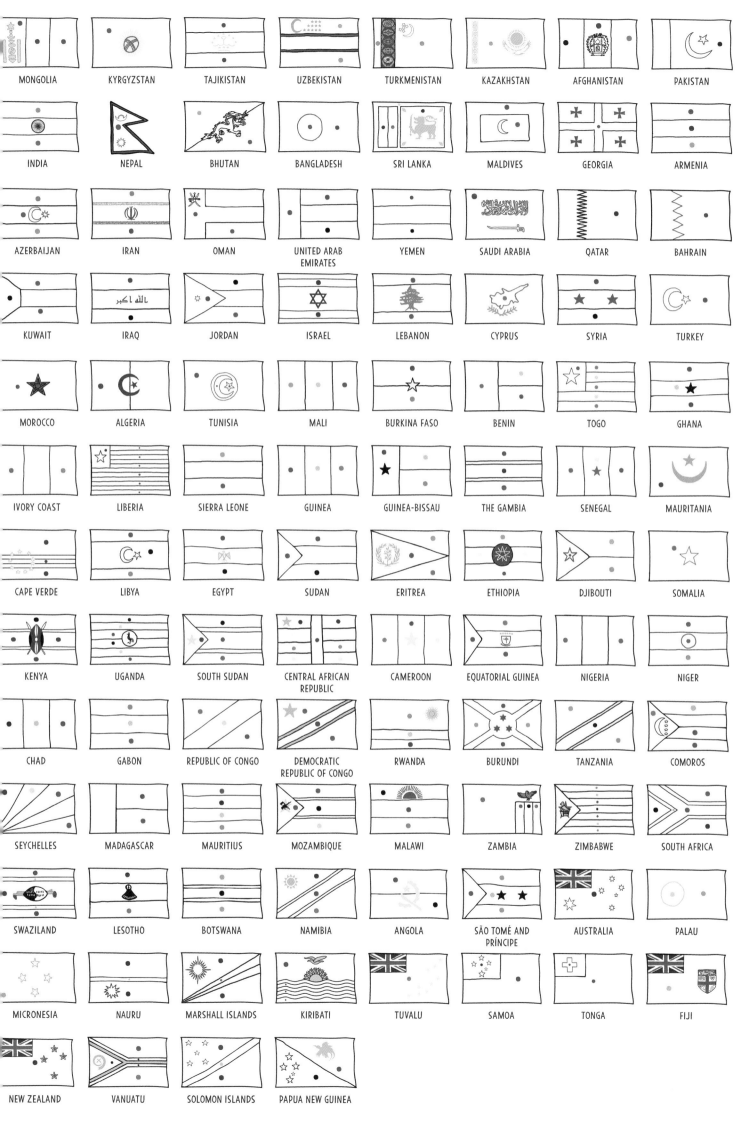

| MONGOLIA | KYRGYZSTAN | TAJIKISTAN | UZBEKISTAN | TURKMENISTAN | KAZAKHSTAN | AFGHANISTAN | PAKISTAN |

| INDIA | NEPAL | BHUTAN | BANGLADESH | SRI LANKA | MALDIVES | GEORGIA | ARMENIA |

| AZERBAIJAN | IRAN | OMAN | UNITED ARAB EMIRATES | YEMEN | SAUDI ARABIA | QATAR | BAHRAIN |

| KUWAIT | IRAQ | JORDAN | ISRAEL | LEBANON | CYPRUS | SYRIA | TURKEY |

| MOROCCO | ALGERIA | TUNISIA | MALI | BURKINA FASO | BENIN | TOGO | GHANA |

| IVORY COAST | LIBERIA | SIERRA LEONE | GUINEA | GUINEA-BISSAU | THE GAMBIA | SENEGAL | MAURITANIA |

| CAPE VERDE | LIBYA | EGYPT | SUDAN | ERITREA | ETHIOPIA | DJIBOUTI | SOMALIA |

| KENYA | UGANDA | SOUTH SUDAN | CENTRAL AFRICAN REPUBLIC | CAMEROON | EQUATORIAL GUINEA | NIGERIA | NIGER |

| CHAD | GABON | REPUBLIC OF CONGO | DEMOCRATIC REPUBLIC OF CONGO | RWANDA | BURUNDI | TANZANIA | COMOROS |

| SEYCHELLES | MADAGASCAR | MAURITIUS | MOZAMBIQUE | MALAWI | ZAMBIA | ZIMBABWE | SOUTH AFRICA |

| SWAZILAND | LESOTHO | BOTSWANA | NAMIBIA | ANGOLA | SÃO TOMÉ AND PRÍNCIPE | AUSTRALIA | PALAU |

| MICRONESIA | NAURU | MARSHALL ISLANDS | KIRIBATI | TUVALU | SAMOA | TONGA | FIJI |

| NEW ZEALAND | VANUATU | SOLOMON ISLANDS | PAPUA NEW GUINEA |